MY EARTH BOOK

PUZZLES, PROJECTS, FACTS, AND FUN

WRITTEN BY LINDA SCHWARTZ
ILLUSTRATED BY BEVERLY ARMSTRONG
EDITED BY SHERRI M. BUTTERFIELD

The Learning Works

Copyright © 1991
by

The Learning Works, Inc.
P.O. Box 6187
Santa Barbara, California 93160

Library of Congress Catalog Number: 91-60123
ISBN 0-88160-201-9
LW 153

Printed in the United States of America.
Current Printing (last digit):   10 9 8 7 6 5 4 3 2 1

This Book Belongs To

_____

(name)

Who Cares About the Earth

Contents

Too Much Trash

Each day, people in the United States throw away enough trash to fill 63,000 garbage trucks. If this many garbage trucks were lined up one after another, the line would be almost 250 miles long. It could reach from New York City to Washington, D.C.!

Digging In!

1. On a map of the United States, find New York City and Washington, D.C.

2. On this map, find two other cities that are this same distance apart.

3. A garbage truck is about 20 feet long and 8 feet wide. Using chalk or sticks and string, make a box that is 20 feet long and 8 feet wide. See how many people can stand together inside a box this big.

4. A garbage truck is about 14 feet tall. Use a measuring tape or yardstick to find out how tall you are. How many kids your size would have to be stacked up to reach as high as 14 feet?

Where Does the Trash Come From?

The trash comes from homes and schools. The trash comes from offices and factories. It also comes from stadiums and parks. The trash is all of the things that kids and grown-ups throw away. Connect the dots to find something that may be part of your trash.

What's in the Trash?

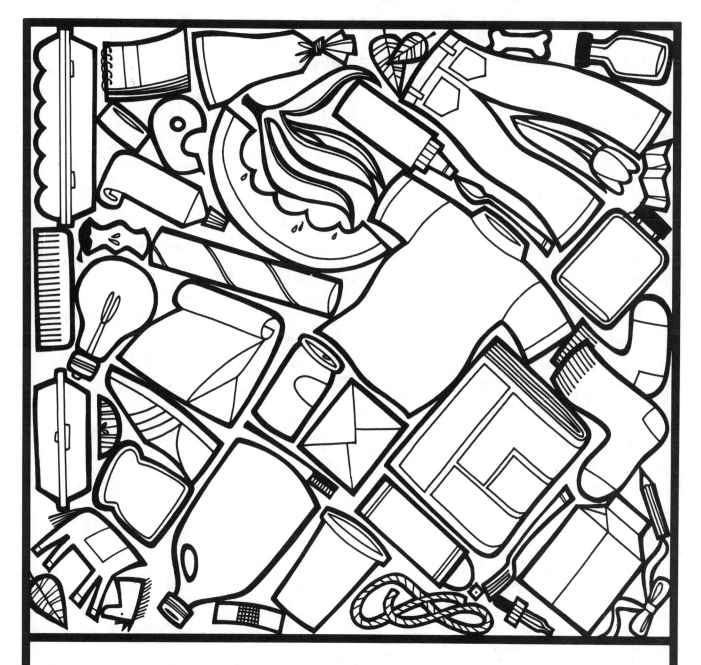

In the trash are apple cores and chicken bones. In the trash are paper plates and cups. In the trash are plastic spoons and forks. In the trash are glass bottles and jars. In the trash are newspapers and cans. In the trash are old furniture and broken toys. Can you find the **bone, cup, fork, jar, can,** and **toy** in this pile of trash?

Turn Trash into Treasure

Instead of throwing away all of your paper trash, save some of it. Turn this trash into a treasured work of art.

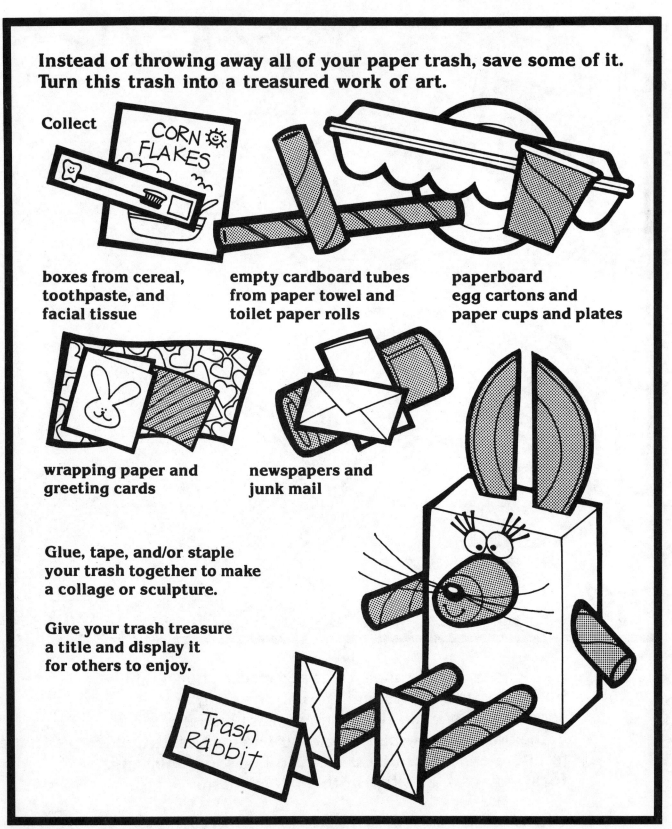

Collect

boxes from cereal, toothpaste, and facial tissue

empty cardboard tubes from paper towel and toilet paper rolls

paperboard egg cartons and paper cups and plates

wrapping paper and greeting cards

newspapers and junk mail

Glue, tape, and/or staple your trash together to make a collage or sculpture.

Give your trash treasure a title and display it for others to enjoy.

Trash Rabbit

The Package Problem

No Wrapping

One Wrapping

in a paper or plastic bag

Two Wrappings

in a paper bag inside a box

Three or More Wrappings

in a plastic bag inside a paperboard box with a foil paper label

One reason there is so much trash is the way things are packaged. For example, some frozen foods are bagged, boxed, and wrapped. First, they are sealed in a plastic bag. Next, they are placed in a paperboard box. Finally, they are wrapped with a foil paper label. When you buy these frozen foods, they are sacked in paper or plastic so you can carry them home. The plastic bag, paperboard box, foil paper label, and grocery sack all end up in the trash.

A Package Hunt

No Wrapping	**One Wrapping**
☐	☐
Two Wrappings	**Three or More Wrappings**
☐	☐

The next time you are in a grocery store or supermarket, go on a package hunt. Count the foods you find with no wrapping, with just one wrapping, with two wrappings, and with three or more wrappings. Draw and color an example of each. Write the number you found in the box.

A Perfect Package

Choose a food that has several wrappings. Draw a new package for this food using fewer wrappings. Be sure that your new package will encourage shoppers to buy the food and keep it fresh.

Where Does the Trash Go?

Garbage trucks take the trash to large open pits called **landfills**. The trash is dumped into these pits and covered with dirt. As more and more trash is dumped and covered, the pile of trash and dirt grows bigger and bigger. Soon it fills the pit. When the pit is full and nothing more can be dumped into it, the landfill must be closed.

Half of the landfills in the United States will be full in less than 10 years. Then where will the trash go?

Digging In!

1. Call your garbage company or department of sanitation to find out where garbage trucks take the trash from your home or school.

2. If your trash goes to a landfill, find out where it is and when it is expected to close.

3. If possible, visit a landfill. While you are there, use your eyes, ears, and nose carefully. When you return to your home or school, make a list of words that tell how a landfill looks, sounds, and smells.

How the Trash Travels

Guide the trash truck from your neighborhood to the nearest landfill. Use a pencil to mark the shortest route for this truck to follow.

What Is Litter?

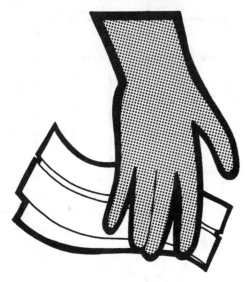

Litter is trash that has been carelessly dropped instead of being placed in a wastebasket or garbage can.

Paper dropped in a city street is litter.

Aluminum cans tossed beside a highway are litter.

Glass bottles left behind at a playground or park are litter.

Cut Open Those Rings!

Don't let the plastic rings that hold six-packs of soda become litter. They are dangerous. Birds, fish, and other animals get caught in them and cannot get out. Cut open those rings before you throw them away. Place the plastic pieces in a trash can or recycle them.

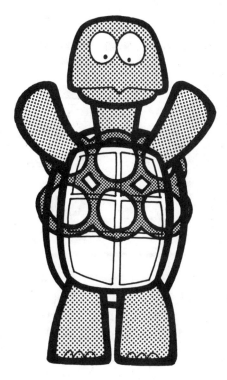

Digging In!

1. Look carefully at one of these plastic six-pack holders. Count the number of holes.

2. Notice the different sizes and shapes of the holes. Name some animals that could get a head, neck, body, or leg caught in these holes.

3. Try to tear one of these plastic six-pack holders apart. How hard must you pull? Could a trapped animal pull hard enough to swim, walk, or fly away?

4. Using a six-pack holder as a pattern, draw a design on a separate sheet of paper. Color your design. Write a title, poem, or message to go with it.

What Is Recycling?

Repackaging is one way to reduce the amount of trash that must be trucked to landfills. Recycling is another way.

Recycling is treating things that have been used so that they can be used again.

Recycling is turning used paper back into pulp and then making new paper from that pulp.

Recycling is crushing used glass bottles into small pieces and melting them to make new glass.

Recycling is melting used aluminum cans, pressing the melted metal into sheets, and shaping these sheets into new cans.

Reasons to Recycle

Recycling saves landfill space because it reduces the amount of trash that must be thrown away.

Recycling saves air and water. It does not dirty them as much as making new products from scratch.

Recycling saves other natural resources like aluminum and trees. Fewer new trees must be cut when used paper is recycled.

Recycling saves energy. Less energy is needed to recycle used products into new ones than to make new products from scratch.

Ways You Can
Reuse and Recycle

Write on both sides of a sheet of paper, not just on one side.

Reuse paper lunch bags or carry your meal in a fabric bag or a lunch box.

Save newspapers and aluminum cans and take them to a recycling center.

When possible, use cloth napkins instead of paper ones.

Wash and reuse glass jars.

Save and reuse gift wrap, or wrap gifts in the comic section of your Sunday newspaper.

Recycling Chart

How many of these items do you reuse and/or recycle? Count them each day for one week. Write the numbers in the boxes. At the end of the week, add the numbers to find your totals.

Item	Day of the Week							Total
	Monday	Tuesday	Wednesday	Thursday	Friday	Saturday	Sunday	
sheets of writing paper or gift wrap								
paper lunch bags								
glass bottles and jars								
daily newspapers								
aluminum cans								
cardboard boxes								
plastic produce bags								
paper or plastic grocery bags								

Recycled Cup Puppets

WHAT YOU NEED

- ☐ used paper cups, rinsed and dried
- ☐ a pencil
- ☐ glue
- ☐ tape
- ☐ a stapler and staples
- ☐ crayons or felt-tipped marking pens
- ☐ recycled odds and ends, such as

  - ☐ construction paper
  - ☐ brads
  - ☐ cotton balls
  - ☐ fabric scraps
  - ☐ feathers

  - ☐ felt
  - ☐ paper clips
  - ☐ pieces of yarn
  - ☐ pipe cleaners
  - ☐ toothpicks

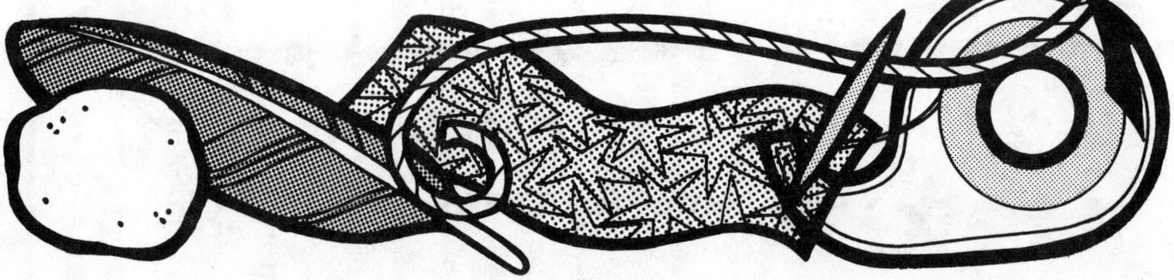

Recycled Cup Puppets
(continued)

YOU CAN MAKE

A MONSTER

TALKING PUPPETS

A CATERPILLAR

BIRDS OR BATS

Work with one cup by itself or fasten several cups together. Use odds and ends to add eyes, nose, mouth, wings, hair, arms, legs, and feet. Give your recycled cup puppet a name.

Paper Bag Vests

WHAT YOU NEED

☐ a large brown paper grocery bag

☐ a pencil

☐ a ruler

☐ scissors

☐ glue

☐ crayons or felt-tipped marking pens

☐ leftover bits of braid, construction paper, fabric, felt, rick-rack, or wrapping paper

WHAT YOU DO

1. Using a pencil and ruler, draw a straight line up the middle of the front or back of the grocery bag.

2. Carefully cut along this line.

Paper Bag Vests
(continued)

3. On the bottom of the bag, draw a circle large enough to go around your neck. Keep the circle small. Don't let it touch the edges of the bottom.

4. Cut out this circle.

5. Cut square holes in the sides for your arms.

6. Try on your vest. Make it fit better. Trim the vest to make it shorter. Cut the neck or armholes larger.

7. Fringe or scallop the bottom of the vest.

8. If there are words on your grocery bag, glue a piece of paper over them.

9. Decorate your vest. Draw on it with crayons or felt-tipped pens. Glue bits of braid, felt, or rick-rack to it.

10. Write a slogan on your vest reminding people to reuse and recycle.

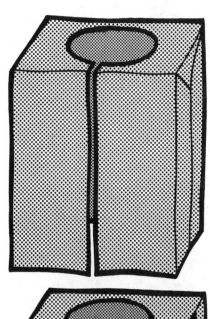

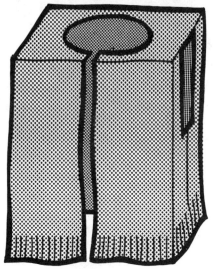

Symbol Search

Many companies want to save our forests. These companies do not cut down trees. They do not make things from wood pulp. Instead, they use recycled paper.

This symbol is printed on packages and other products made from recycled paper. The next time you are in a supermarket or card shop, go on a symbol search. See if you can find this symbol on a bag, box, or card. Write about what you find on the lines below.

I found this symbol on a _____

in _____.

(name of store)

Whose Home?

Recycling paper saves trees. Recycling paper also saves the homes of animals that live in trees. To find the animal that lives in this tree, color the shapes that have dots on them. Can you think of another animal whose home is in a tree?

Animals in Danger

The total number of some kinds of animals stays the same or gets larger. The total number of other kinds of animals grows smaller. These animals are in danger of dying out completely, or becoming **extinct**. They are in danger for many reasons.

People destroy their homes.

Birds and squirrels die because people cut down the trees in which they nest or the forests in which they hide.

People poison them.

Many California condors died after eating poisoned meat put out by ranchers to kill coyotes.

Fish die in rivers that have been poisoned by dirty water from homes and factories.

Animals in Danger

People hunt them.

Hawksbill turtles are killed for their shells.

African elephants are hunted and killed for the ivory in their tusks.

People collect them.

The thick-billed parrot is caught and sold to pet shops.

Endangered Animals

grizzly bear

Guadalupe fur seal

Galapagos tortoise

Schaus swallowtail butterfly

Endangered Animals

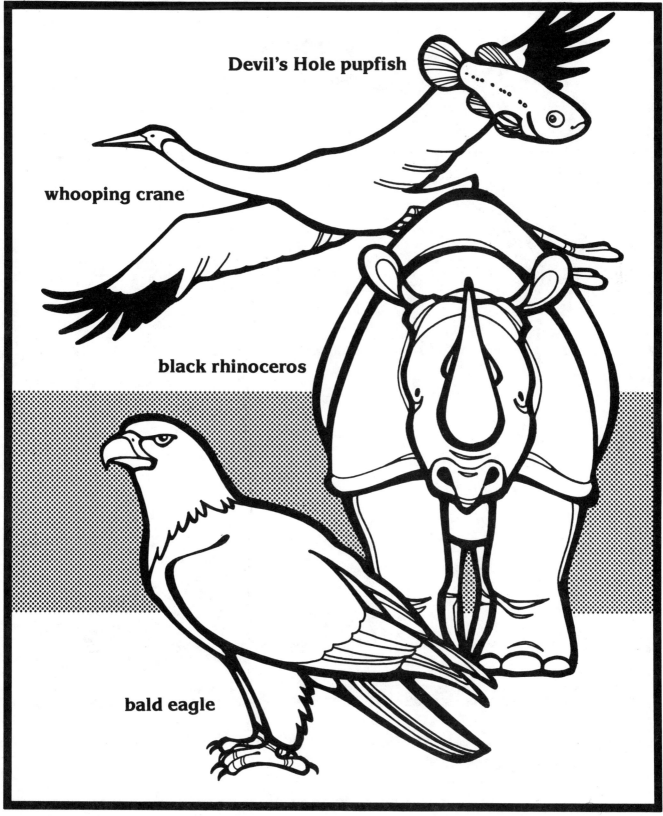

Devil's Hole pupfish

whooping crane

black rhinoceros

bald eagle

Who's in Danger?

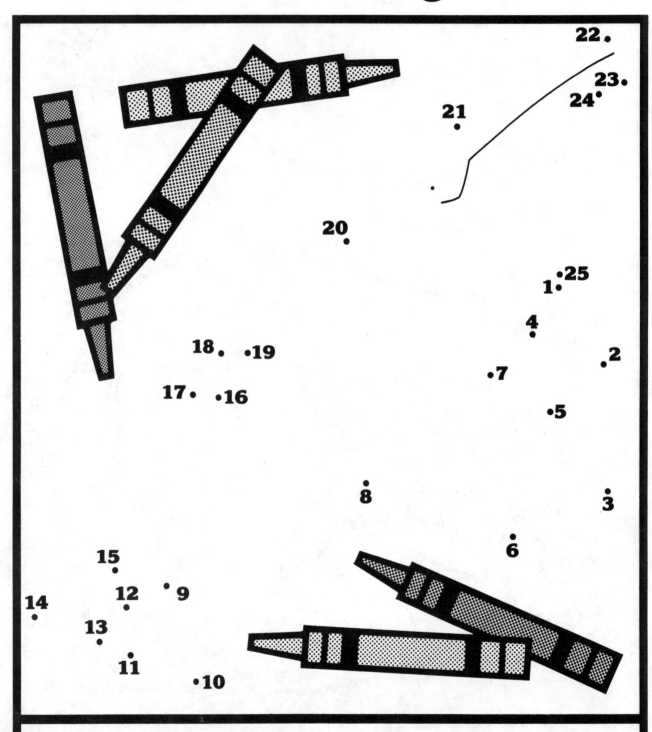

Connect the dots to draw a picture of another animal in danger. Color the animal.

The Burrowing Owl

Burrowing owls are found in the grasslands and deserts of North, Central, and South America. They build nests in holes left empty by prairie dogs and tortoises. These brown and white birds eat insects, lizards, and mice.

Burrowing owls are in danger. Farmers are destroying their homes and poisoning their food. Plowing damages their burrows. Spraying poisons the insects and mice they eat.

Make a Mobile

1. **Reuse some brown paper lunch bags to make a colony of burrowing owls.**

2. **Using a black crayon or felt-tipped marking pen, draw eyes and beaks on the bags.**

3. **Tape or glue on construction paper legs.**

4. **Using string or thread, hang the owls from a wire coat hanger, wooden dowel, or tree branch.**

You Can Make
A Milk Carton Bird Feeder

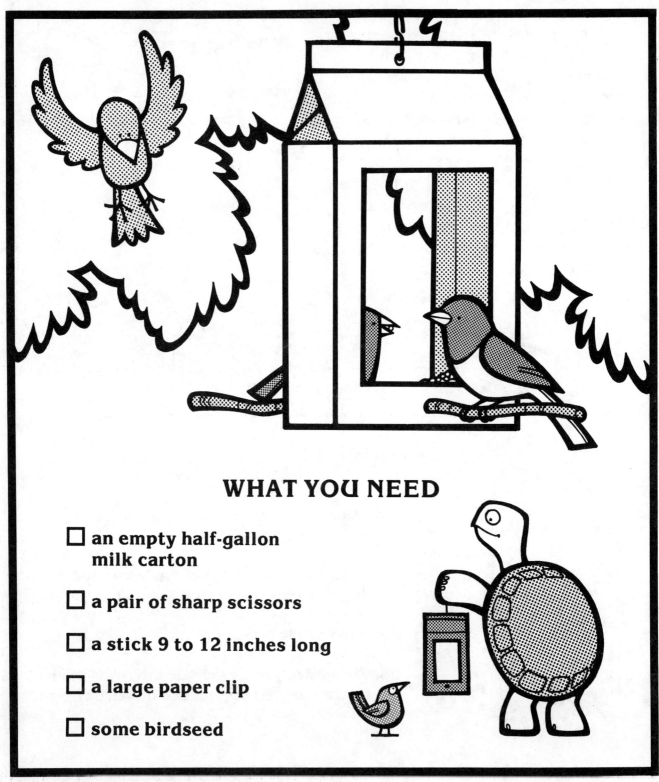

WHAT YOU NEED

- [ ] an empty half-gallon milk carton

- [ ] a pair of sharp scissors

- [ ] a stick 9 to 12 inches long

- [ ] a large paper clip

- [ ] some birdseed

You Can Make a Milk Carton Bird Feeder
(continued)

WHAT YOU DO

1. Wash and dry the milk carton.

2. Using scissors, cut windows in two sides of the carton, leaving margins as shown.*

3. Carefully cut a small hole in each of the sides near the bottom of the carton.*

4. Run the stick through both of these holes to create a perch.

5. Straighten the paper clip to make a hook.

6. Insert this hook through the top of the milk carton as shown.

7. Put some birdseed on the bottom of the feeder.

8. Hang the feeder outside. Choose a spot where feeding birds will be safe from cats and other animals that sometimes harm birds.

*You may need adult help with these steps.

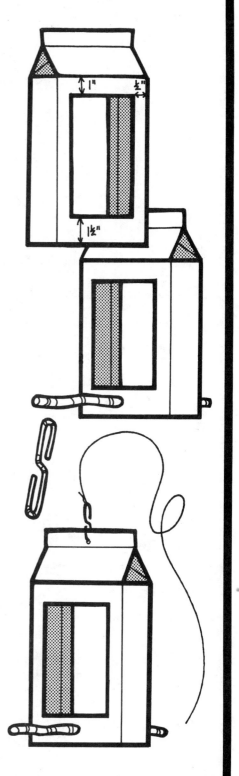

Habitat Match and Color

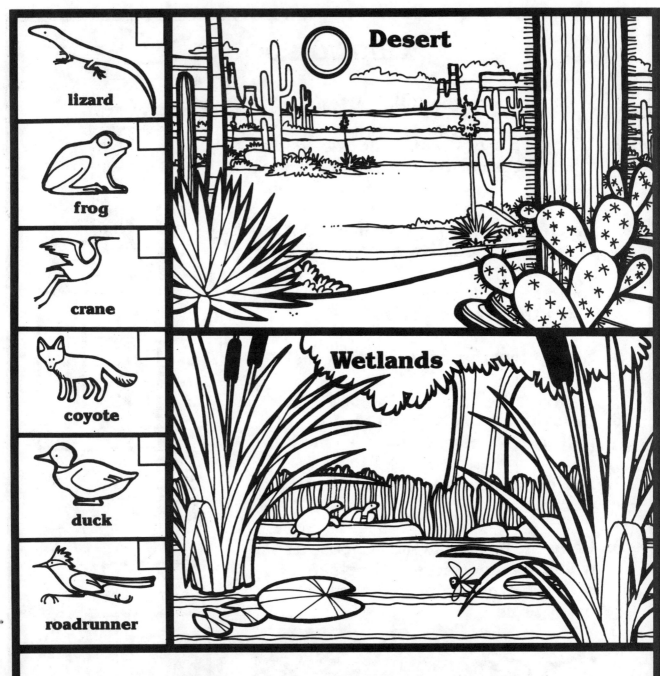

A **habitat** is the place where an animal naturally lives and grows. Habitats provide food, water, shelter, and space. Match the animals to their habitats by writing a letter in each small box. Write either the letter **D** for **Desert** or the letter **W** for **Wetlands**. Color the pictures.

Habitat Match and Color

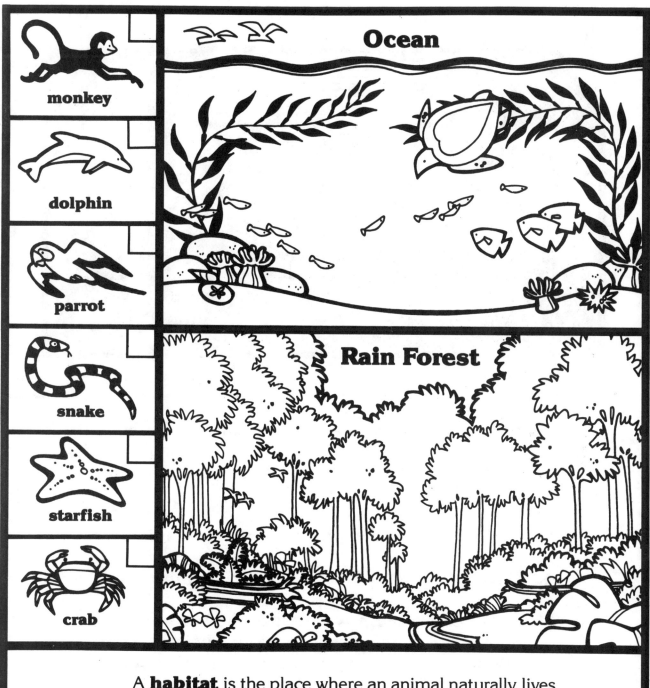

monkey

dolphin

parrot

snake

starfish

crab

Ocean

Rain Forest

A **habitat** is the place where an animal naturally lives and grows. Habitats provide food, water, shelter, and space. Match the animals to their habitats by writing a letter in each small box. Write either the letter **O** for **Ocean** or the letter **R** for **Rain Forest**. Color the pictures.

A Shoe Box Scene

1. **Pick an animal you would like to learn more about.**

2. **Read a book about the habits and habitat of this animal.**

3. **Find five fascinating facts about this animal.**

4. **Write these facts on a white, lined index card.**

5. **Turn an old shoe box into a scene showing this animal in its habitat. Use construction paper cutouts and scrap materials to create this scene.**

6. **Tape or glue the fact card to the top of the shoe box.**

7. **Display your shoe box scene for others to enjoy.**

A Poster to Color

Look, Learn, and Leave It Alone!

When you are enjoying nature, don't collect eggs, disturb nests, or remove animals from their natural habitats.

Did You Know?

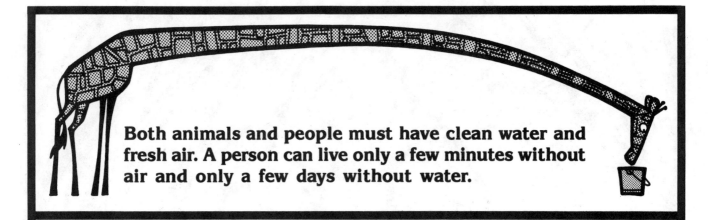

Both animals and people must have clean water and fresh air. A person can live only a few minutes without air and only a few days without water.

Water covers nearly three-fourths of the earth.

Did You Know?

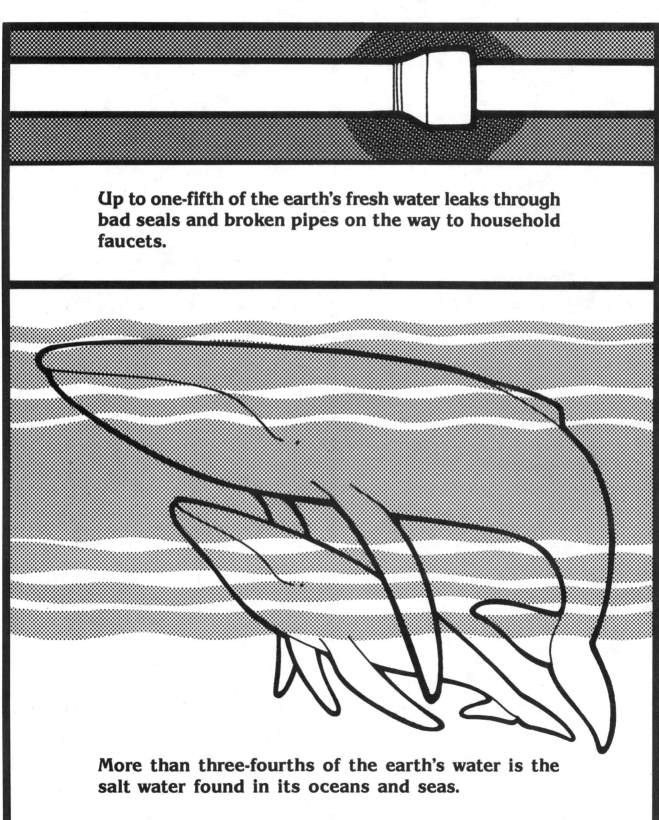

Up to one-fifth of the earth's fresh water leaks through bad seals and broken pipes on the way to household faucets.

More than three-fourths of the earth's water is the salt water found in its oceans and seas.

Ways We Use Water

We use water for cooking.

We use water for cleaning.

We use water for washing clothes and dishes.

We use water for flushing toilets.

Ways We Use Water

We use water for heating and cooling.

We use water to wet lawns and gardens.

We use water to fight fires.

We use water to make electricity.

One Way I Use Water

Draw and color a picture showing one way you use water.

Ways We Waste Water

We waste water by letting the water run while we prerinse dishes or brush our teeth.

We waste water by failing to fix drippy faucets and leaky pipes.

We waste water by letting the water run until it is warm enough for a shower or cold enough for a drink.

We waste water by letting it fall on sidewalks, driveways, and streets when we are watering our gardens and lawns.

One Way I Waste Water

Each person uses about 70 gallons of water a day. Much of this water is wasted. Think about the ways you use water. Draw and color a picture showing one way you waste water.

Stop That Drop!

Leaking faucets waste water. A small drip can waste more than 50 gallons of water a day!

Count the faucets inside your house or apartment. Include faucets that bring water into bathtubs, showers, and sinks. How many did you find? Write the number in this box.

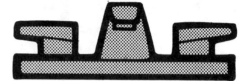

If you found a leaky faucet, put a plastic pitcher under it to catch the drip.

In an hour or so, check to see how much water is in the pitcher. Is the pitcher

almost full,

about half full,

or still empty?

Make good use of the water in the pitcher. Use it to drink, water plants, or wash the car.

Tell your parents about the leaky faucet so they can get it fixed and stop that drop!

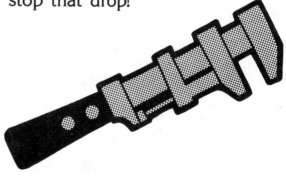

Shorter Showers

A two-minute shower uses about 24 gallons of water.

A full-tub bath uses more than 40 gallons of water.

A ten-minute shower uses over 100 gallons of water.

WHAT YOU CAN DO

1. Take short showers instead of long showers or full baths.

2. Use a three-minute egg timer to time your showers. Try to finish showering before the time is up.

3. Turn off the water while you soap your body and wash your hair. Turn the water back on when you are ready to rinse off the suds.

4. Ask your mom or dad to put in low-flow shower heads. They save water by slowing the water flow from 12 to 3 gallons a minute.

My Earth Book
© 1991—The Learning Works, Inc.

Shorter Showers Chart

Name	Minutes Spent Showering On							Total
	Monday	Tuesday	Wednesday	Thursday	Friday	Saturday	Sunday	

Write the names of the people in your family on this chart. For one week, ask them to time their showers and record the number of minutes each shower takes. At the end of the week, add the minutes and decide who has taken the shortest showers. Give this person a Shortest Showers Award (see page 48).

This

Shortest Showers Award

is given to

_____
(name of winner)

for saving water by spending only _____ *minutes*
(total)

in the shower during one week.

_____
(your name)

_____
(date)

Save a Stream

Fresh water flows in rivers and streams. The clean water in streams can easily get dirty. People drop trash into streams. Farmers spray poisons on their crops. Rains wash these poisons into streams. Broken sewer pipes leak waste water into streams.

Dirty stream water can make animals and people sick. It can even kill the fish and insects that live in streams.

What You Can Do

1. You can be careful about where you throw your trash. Place it in a covered can so that it cannot blow or flow into a stream.

2. You can pick up any paper or plastic trash you find beside a stream so that it will not fall into the water. When you pick up trash, you may want to wear gloves and you should ask a parent, teacher, or other adult for help.

3. For more information and ideas, you can write a letter to

Save Our Streams
The Izaak Walton League of America
1401 Wilson Boulevard, Level B
Arlington, Virginia 22209

Family Fun

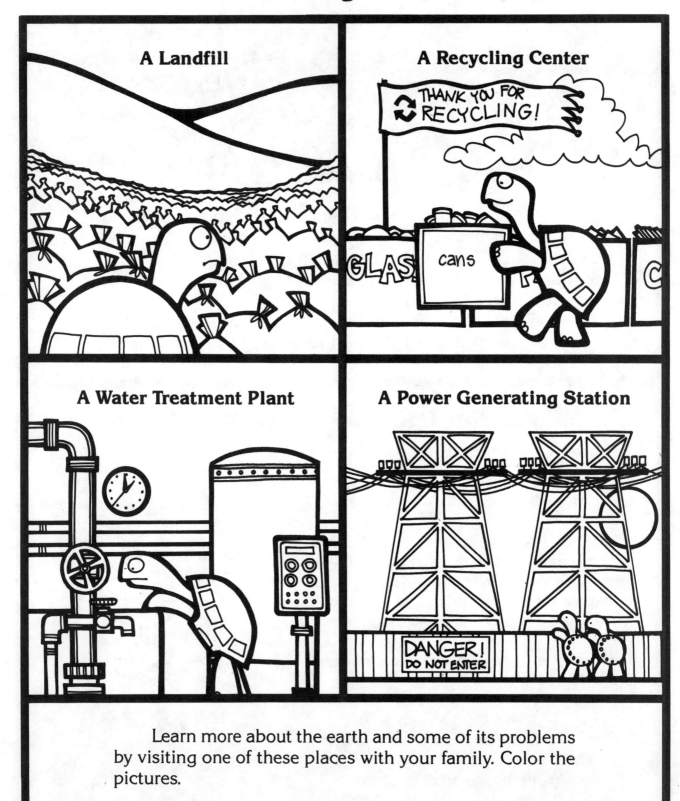

A Landfill

A Recycling Center

THANK YOU FOR RECYCLING!

GLAS   cans

A Water Treatment Plant

A Power Generating Station

DANGER! DO NOT ENTER

Learn more about the earth and some of its problems by visiting one of these places with your family. Color the pictures.

More Family Fun

A Zoo or Nature Center

A River, Pond, or Beach

A Natural History Museum

POLAR BEAR

A National Park

Learn more about the earth and some of its animals by visiting one of these places with your family. Color the pictures.

My Coat of Arms

A coat of arms is a shield. Coats of arms are decorated with pictures and words. Decorate this coat of arms. Use pictures and words that tell what you know and how you feel about your earth.

Tell Your Friends

An Earth Message

Help Animals
Plant Trees
Prevent Forest Fires
Recycle
Save Water

A Special Way to Say It

Bookmark
Bumper Sticker
Lapel Button
Postage Stamp
Poster

Plant a tree for me!

HELP ANIMALS!

UNITED STATES POSTAGE 29¢

Save water!

If you could tell your friends one very important thing about the earth, what would it be? Choose an earth message from the list above or write your own. Then, on a separate sheet of paper, say it in a special way.

What else would you like to tell people about the earth? Can you think of another way to tell them?

Create an Award

This
**Water
Drop
Medal**
is presented to

_____
(name)
for replacing
the faucet washer
and stopping
the drip.

This
Space Saver Award
is presented to

_____
(name)
for saving landfill space by recycling aluminum, glass, and paper.

RECYCLE!

This
Super Scissors Certificate
is presented to

_____
(name)
for carefully cutting open all of the loops in the plastic rings used to package six-packs of soda so that animals cannot get caught in them.

Create an award to give to someone who has done something good for the earth. This award can be a ribbon, a medal, or a certificate. It can be given for recycling paper, saving water, planting trees, or doing anything else that helps the earth.

Game Instructions

1. Cut out the game cards on pages 57 through 61.
2. Color the cards if you wish.
3. Use the cards as they are or glue them to cardboard or tagboard to make them stronger.
4. Shuffle the cards and stack them face down.
5. One at a time, draw a card from the stack.
6. Turn the card over.
7. Read the statement on the card carefully.
8. Decide if the statement is true or false.
9. If the statement is true, put the card in the box marked **true**. If the statement is false, put the card in the box marked **false**.
10. When you have read each card and put it in a box, check your answers. Use the answer key on page 56.

Play this game with family members or friends. If there is more than one player, players should take turns drawing cards and should each create their own true and false stacks. When all of the cards are gone, the winner is the player who has the most cards correctly stacked.

Game Answer Key

1. True (page 12).

2. True (pages 24–25). More than 500,000 trees are used each week to produce Sunday newspapers.

3. True (pages 26–27). Some animals are in danger of becoming extinct because people hunt them, collect them, destroy their homes, and poison them.

4. False (page 12). The United States is running out of landfill space. Half of the landfills in this country will be full in less than 10 years.

5. False (page 38). Water covers **more** than half of the earth.

6. False (page 17). **Less** energy is needed to recycle used products into new ones than to make new products from scratch.

7. False (page 27). Hawksbill turtles are killed for their **shells**. African elephants are killed for their ivory tusks.

8. True (page 24).

9. False (page 14). **Litter** is trash that has been carelessly dropped instead of being placed in a wastebasket or garbage can.

10. True (page 16).

11. False (pages 16–17). Aluminum, glass, paper, and plastic trash and yard cuttings can all be recycled.

12. True (page 31).

13. False (page 45). Even a small drip can waste more than 50 gallons of water a day. That's enough water to fill 800 eight-ounce glasses!

14. False (page 16). Glass, aluminum, and plastic can also be recycled.

15. True (page 26).

16. False (page 34). A **habitat** is the place where an animal naturally lives and grows.

17. True (page 34).

18. True (page 17).

19. False (page 34). Wetlands are the natural home of cranes, ducks, frogs, and many other animals.

20. False (page 15). Birds, fish, and other animals get caught in these rings and cannot tear or break the plastic to free themselves.

21. False (page 38). Both animals and people need fresh water. In fact, a person can live only a few days without it.

22. True (page 44).

23. False (page 37). It is not good to keep wild animals as pets. The best way to enjoy nature is to look, learn, and leave it alone.

24. False (page 16). During the recycling process, old glass is crushed into small pieces, melted, and made into new glass.

1. Garbage trucks take trash to large open pits called **landfills**.

2. Recycling paper saves trees.

3. Some animals are in danger of becoming extinct.

4. Because the United States is a big country, it will never run out of landfill space.

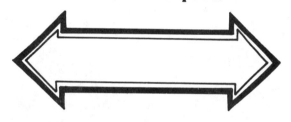

5. Water covers less than half of the earth.

6. More energy is needed to recycle used products into new ones than to make new products from scratch.

7. People kill hawksbill turtles for their ivory tusks.

8. This symbol is printed on bags and boxes made from recycled paper.

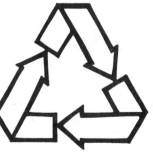

© 1991—The Learning Works, Inc.

© 1991—The Learning Works, Inc.

© 1991—The Learning Works, Inc.

© 1991—The Learning Works, Inc.

© 1991—The Learning Works, Inc.

© 1991—The Learning Works, Inc.

© 1991—The Learning Works, Inc.

© 1991—The Learning Works, Inc.

9. **Litter** is trash that has been carefully placed in wastebaskets or garbage cans.

10. **Recycling** is treating things that have been used so that they can be used again.

11. All of our trash must be thrown away because none of it can be recycled.

12. Burrowing owls are in danger because people destroy their homes and poison their food.

13. A drippy faucet cannot waste more than one glass of water a day.

14. Only newspapers, magazines, and other paper products can be recycled.

15. Dirty water from homes and factories can poison rivers and kill the fish that live in them.

16. **A habitat** is one animal that is in danger of becoming extinct.

17. A roadrunner's natural habitat is the desert.

18. Recycling saves air, water, energy, and natural resources.

19. Wetlands are messy, muddy places where no animals live.

20. Because plastic six-pack rings bend easily, they cannot harm animals in any way.

21. Fresh water is nice to have, but people and animals can live without it.

NO WATER? NO PROBLEM!

22. Each person uses about 70 gallons of water a day.

23. One way people can protect wild animals is to catch them and keep them as pets.

24. Because glass is hard and breaks easily, it cannot be recycled.

Answer Key

Page 6, Where Does the Trash Come From?
The picture is of a tennis shoe.

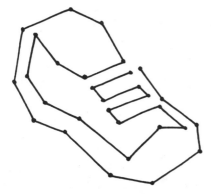

Page 7, What's in the Trash?

Page 13, How the Trash Travels

Page 25, Whose Home?
The animal that lives in this tree is a squirrel.

Page 30, Who's in Danger?
The picture is of a whale.

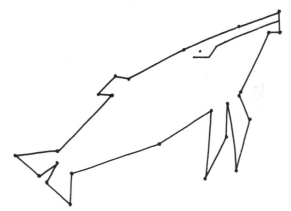

Page 34, Habitat Match and Color
The coyote, lizard, and roadrunner live in the desert.
The crane, duck, and frog live in the wetlands.

Page 35, Habitat Match and Color
The crab, dolphin, and starfish live in the ocean.
The monkey, parrot, and snake live in the rain forest.

OTHER ENVIRONMENTAL ACTIVITY BOOKS
FOR KIDS FROM THE LEARNING WORKS

The Learning Works
EARTH BOOK FOR KIDS

ACTIVITIES TO HELP
HEAL THE ENVIRONMENT

WRITTEN BY LINDA SCHWARTZ · ILLUSTRATED BY BEVERLY ARMSTRONG

LW 289
ISBN 0-88160-195-0
9" × 8¼" — 184 pages
Softbound

Creative ideas with easy-to-follow instructions show kids how to
• *make their own paper* • *compare phosphate levels in detergents* • *test the effects of oil pollution* • *conduct a recycling survey* • *create a trash sculpture* • *redesign a package* • *and make a difference in many other exciting ways.*

An Exciting Collection of Earth-Friendly Activities Created Especially for Kids!

Earth Book for Kids offers children a wide variety of ways to learn about the environment while having fun. It is filled with ideas for art activities, craft projects, experiments, explorations, and experiences that will encourage children to enjoy and heal the environment. (Grades 4–6)

Earth Book for Kids covers

• acid rain
• air and water pollution
• deforestation
• endangered wildlife
• energy and resource conservation
• landfills and litter
• packaging
• pesticides
• recycling
• many other related topics

$9.95

Endangered Wildlife

LW 803 COMPREHENSION COLLECTION

Exciting stories about fourteen endangered animals with follow-up questions that emphasize developing vocabulary, finding facts, recognizing the main idea, and drawing conclusions. Bonus projects include poster and mural making, creative writing, and critical thinking. (Grades 4–6)

$3.95

Language and Math Games Using Recycled Containers

LW 115 GARBAGE GAMES
Make recycling a habit! Follow simple instructions to transform empty boxes, cans, cartons, and wrappers into creative games to teach language arts and math. Includes games for vowels, consonants, syllables, antonyms, synonyms, parts of speech, vocabulary, punctuation, spelling, and more.

$9.95

SAMPLE EXERCISES
• Soup Sums
• Pizza Plus
• Egg-sactly Right
• Paper Dolls
• Nuts-and-Bolts Numbers

(Grades 1–4)

Explore the World of Animals!

LW 266 BIRDS
LW 267 MAMMALS
LW 268 FISHES
LW 269 REPTILES

$3.95 each

Each value-priced book contains descriptions of fourteen animals with full-page, detailed illustrations suitable for coloring. Follow-up activities offer practice in design, research, math, vocabulary, and writing skills. Each book includes games, puzzles, and an illustrated "facts" page. (Grades 1–6)

Order from your favorite bookstore, school supply dealer, or from The Learning Works.